The Fruit Of The Spirit

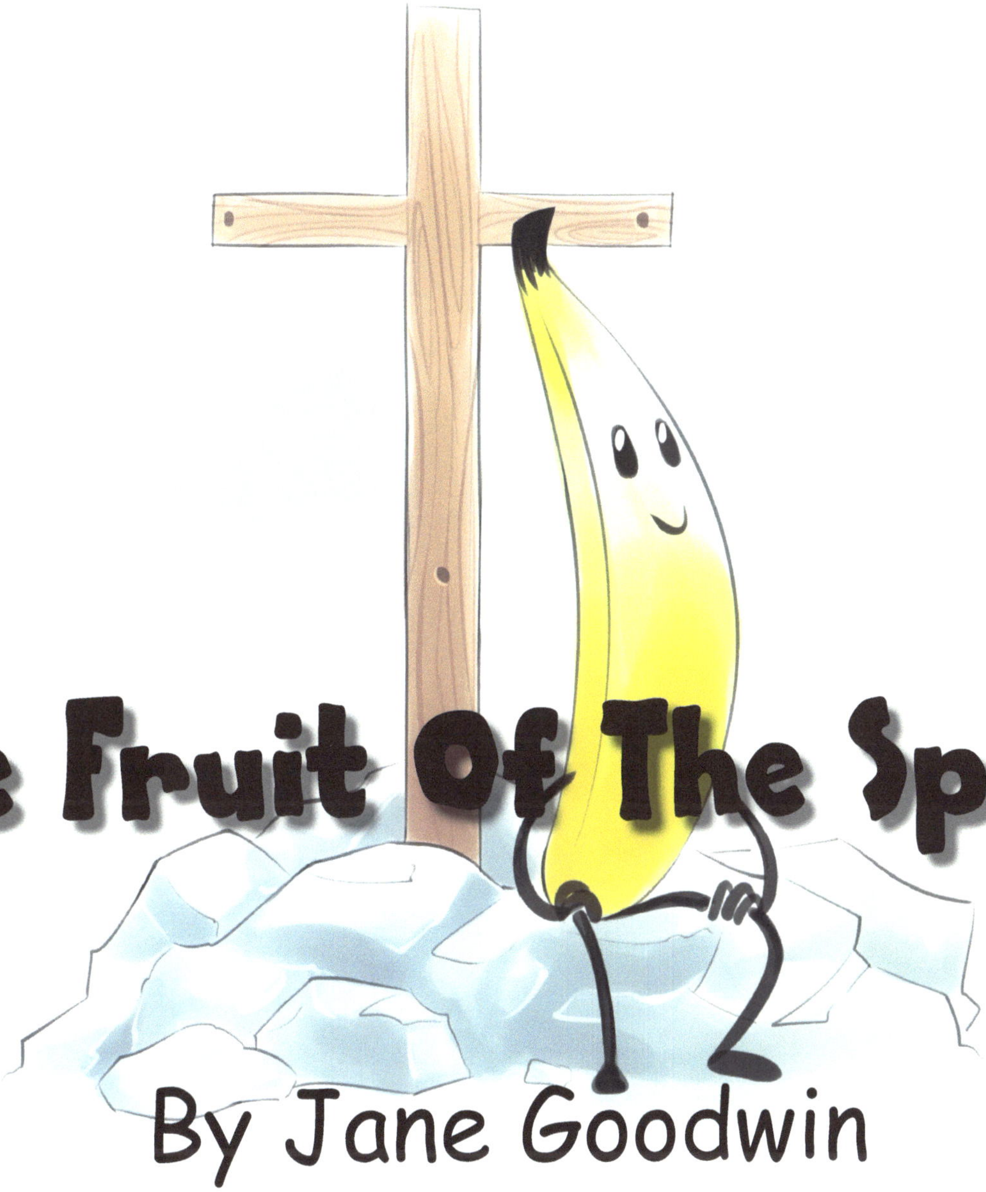

By Jane Goodwin

Illustrations by Eric Toner

The Fruit Of The Spirit

Written and designed by Jane Goodwin

Illustrations by Eric Toner

Published in Canada by Worship With Us Ministries
International Standard Book Number: 978-1-7752467-3-2

www.worshipwithus.ca/books

BUT THE FRUIT OF THE SPIRIT IS

LOVE

JOY

PEACE

PATIENCE

KINDNESS

GOODNESS

FAITHFULNESS

GENTLENESS

SELF CONTROL

AGAINST SUCH THINGS THERE IS NO LAW

GALATIANS 5: 22-23

LOVE

LOVE is not a feeling but it is a choice. We can choose to be kind, to put other's needs before our own. Even when we meet someone we don't like or who doesn't like us we can choose to love them anyway.

Jesus came with love for everyone, even the ones who didn't love him. We can do the same, by choosing to love those who are not so loveable because Jesus is **LOVE**.

"But now faith, hope, LOVE, abide these three; but the greatest of these is LOVE."
1 Corinthians 13:13

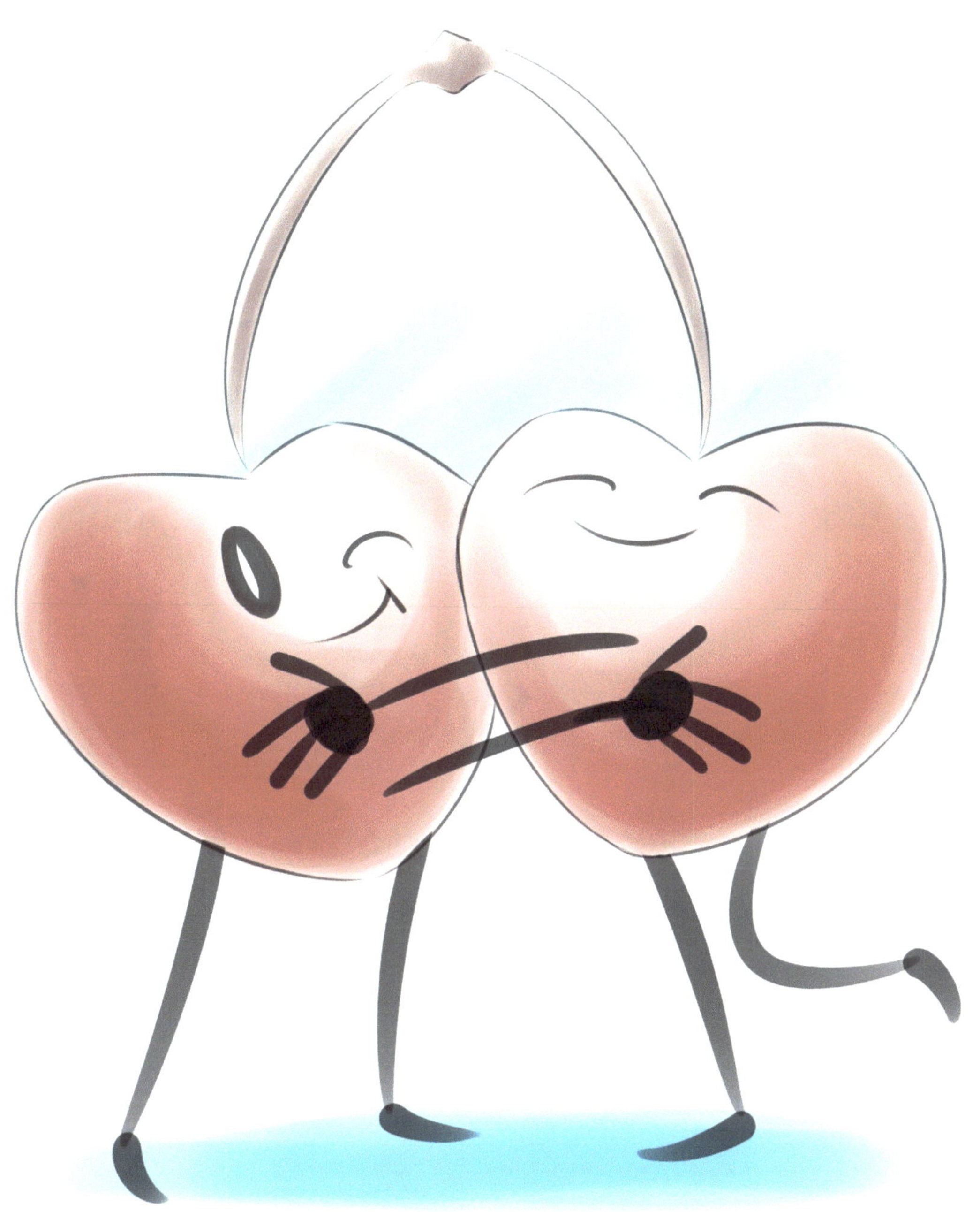

JOY

JOY is a feeling of great happiness inside us. It happens when we see someone or something we like or love a lot. God's heart is full of joy when He sees us. When we learn how great, how wonderful and how loving our God is, it in turn fills our hearts with a bubbly, exciting feeling of joy. We need to know Jesus is our **JOY**.

"These things I have spoken to you so that My JOY may be in you, and that your JOY may be made full."
John 15:11

PEACE

PEACE is when we are able to rest without fear, trust without doubt, love without strings, quietness, calm and contentment. God is the one who gives us peace. Peace in our minds, our bodies, our souls and our spirits. Jesus is called the Prince of Peace. He is the one who brings his peace into our lives as we rest, trust, love, calm ourselves and are content to be His child. Jesus is our **PEACE**.

"These things I have spoken to you, so that in Me you may have PEACE**. In the world you have tribulation, but take courage; I have overcome the world."**
John 16:33

PATIENCE

PATIENCE is what we use when we have to wait for things we want. Patience is also what we use when someone is not as fast, or as smart, or as happy as we are. Patience is not getting angry when things are not going our way. In everything that happens we can ask Jesus to show us how to be patient through it all. Jesus is **PATIENT**.

"With all humility and gentleness, with **PATIENCE**, showing tolerance for one another in love."
Ephesians 4:2

KINDNESS

KINDNESS is being good to others. When we see someone fall, it is kind to help them up. When someone loses something, it is KIND to help them find it. When someone is hungry it is kind to share some food with them. When someone is sad, it is kind to give them a hug. Kindness is doing good things for others. Jesus was always kind to others. Jesus is **KIND**.

"So, as those who have been chosen of God, holy and beloved, put on a heart of compassion, KINDNESS, humility, gentleness and patience."
Colossians 3:12

GOODNESS

GOODNESS is the best part of anything. When we are loving and joyful. When we are at peace and we are patient. When we are kind, full of faith, gentleness and self-control, we show others who God is. We show them His goodness that He has placed in us. We show others the very best of God and the very best of us.

This is what Jesus did while He was here on earth. Jesus is **GOOD**.

"Surely GOODNESS and loving kindness will follow me all the days of my life, and I will dwell in the house of the Lord forever."

Psalm 23:6

FAITHFULNESS

FAITHFULNESS is our continued trust, belief, and love for God, His son Jesus and the Holy Spirit. It does not matter what is going on in our lives. To be faithful we continue to trust in God, believe what His word says and love Him with all our hearts. We are each given a measure of faith from God, and as we are faithful to Him, He shows His faithfulness to us. Jesus is **FAITHFUL**.

"God is FAITHFUL, through whom you were called into fellowship with His Son, Jesus Christ our Lord."
1 Corinthians 1:9

GENTLENESS

GENTLENESS is being kind and careful. It is the way someone acts when they are soft and calm and sweet to other people. It shows itself in humility, that is not thinking you are better than other people, but being concerned, polite and loving toward others. When a daddy holds a tiny baby, he is very gentle not to hurt or scare the baby. This is a picture of how God is with his children and how we are called to be with others. Jesus is **GENTLE**.

"Let your GENTLE spirit be known to all men. The Lord is near."
Philippians 4:5

SELF-CONTROL

SELF-CONTROL IS being able to say no to things that we really know are not good or right for us. It also means being able to tell when we have had enough. Just the right amount of ice cream makes us feel good. Too much ice cream will make us feel very sick. When we have the fruit of self-control, we are able to control what we think, what we say and what we do. We are more like Jesus.

Jesus had, and He helps us, with **SELF-CONTROL.**

"Now for this very reason also, applying all diligence, in your faith supply moral excellence, and in your moral excellence, knowledge, and in your knowledge, **SELF-CONTROL**, and in your **SELF-CONTROL**, perseverance, and in your perseverance, godliness, and in your godliness, brotherly kindness, and in your brotherly kindness, love."
2 Peter 1: 5-7

JESUS GROWS THE FRUIT

All of the fruit of the Spirit can be ours. We just need to ask Jesus to grow and cultivate His fruit in our lives and let Him teach us to walk in His ways. As we grow we will develop more and more of His fruit and live the life He has called us to live.

A life filled with **LOVE, JOY, PEACE, PATIENCE, KINDNESS, GOODNESS, FAITHFULNESS, GENTLENESS, and SELF-CONTROL.**

www.ingramcontent.com/pod-product-compliance
Ingram Content Group UK Ltd.
Pitfield, Milton Keynes, MK11 3LW, UK
UKHW060115300726
14090UKWH00002B/210

* 9 7 8 1 7 7 5 2 4 6 7 3 2 *